Also by the same Author
A Simple Guide to Voyaging the Energetic Universe

ISBN: 978-1-291-96031-0 (sc)
ISBN: 978-1-4834-1871-1(e)

The Multi-Dimensional Voyager

How the Voyager becomes the Wizard,
Master of Dimension and Time

Michael Webster

Copyright © 2016 Michael Webster.

Image credit: michael webster

All rights reserved. No part of this book may be reproduced, stored, or transmitted by any means—whether auditory, graphic, mechanical, or electronic—without written permission of both publisher and author, except in the case of brief excerpts used in critical articles and reviews. Unauthorized reproduction of any part of this work is illegal and is punishable by law.

ISBN: 978-1-4834-5049-0 (sc)
ISBN: 978-1-4834-5050-6 (e)

Because of the dynamic nature of the Internet, any web addresses or links contained in this book may have changed since publication and may no longer be valid. The views expressed in this work are solely those of the author and do not necessarily reflect the views of the publisher, and the publisher hereby disclaims any responsibility for them.

Any people depicted in stock imagery provided by Thinkstock are models, and such images are being used for illustrative purposes only.
Certain stock imagery © Thinkstock.

Lulu Publishing Services rev. date: 04/15/2016

Dedication

This book is dedicated to our students without whom the development and expansion of our work would not have happened.

To my grandchildren Harris, Harry, Emily, Ailis, Cian, Hannah and Bethany who have the chance to make this beautiful world an even better place to live in.

Finally to my lovely wife Stella with my eternal gratitude for love, support, faith and encouragement. Together through everything.

Contents

Acknowledgements ix
Foreword xi
Introduction xiii

    1) Mastery - A Continuous Process 1
    2) The Intelligent, Self-Aware Universe 3
    3) Me-Self-I 8
    4) On Letting Go! 11
    5) Enlightenment – Whatever that means to you! 19
    6) Stepping Into The Void 24
    7) Ordinary and Enlightened. 28
    8) Manifesting the Mirror. 31
    9) The Enigma of Time 34
    10) Bi-location – Somewhere in time? 40
    11) Through the Veil of Death 46
    12) The Wizard and Advanced Fingerprinting 51
    13) The Power of the Wizard 59

Epilogue - Treading the Path of the Masters 63
References 69
Appendix 71
Glossary 75
Training in Waveform 79
The Author 81

Acknowledgements

As with any work of a similar kind, the insights contained are more than just the work and experience of the author's life. Many people wittingly and unwittingly play a part in creating the circumstances from which development and insight arise. This book is no different.

Our students come from many walks of life; from different backgrounds; different cultures; asking different questions; having different experiences. This wonderful mix has stoked the fires of investigation, experimentation, learning and experience. The Energetic Matrix has provided us with the means to grow, expand and understand once we had learned, absorbed and integrated our earlier lessons.

In recent times my own lessons from the universe often appear un-announced in mid-workshop, setting an energetic puzzle for me to work out before I set one for the students. The universe has a sense of humour it seems.

Our venues have added to the development and learning experience: Holycombe in Warwickshire, England, Duck Bay Hotel by Loch Lomond, Scotland, Spirit Matters, Ontario, Canada, Kumbali Country Lodge in Malawi and the International Academy for Hara Shiatsu in Vienna are just a few of the wonderful venues we have used over the years. They have been far more than 'just a venue' to us, so I say to them please accept my thanks for the many ways you have contributed to and enhanced our workshops in the past and we look forward to a long future association with you.

To the team, as always supportive, Nicky, Erici, Jean-Gil, Wulf, Miriam and Kerry. To Martin Armitage-Smith for agreeing to find the stamina to edit and make readable another of my tomes and to my son Michael for creating the cover and back pages. My heart-felt thanks to you all. My thanks to all our students across the globe from whom I learn more and more.

To the universe, a source of wonder, motivation, and a constant and patient teacher, without which this book would not be written. My deep gratitude.

Finally to Stella, who embodies the compassion and spirit of the Universe, my love and eternal gratitude.

Mike Webster 22nd July 2015.

Foreword

I feel privileged to have been asked to write a foreword for Mike's second book.

Since I first met Mike via email during my early Shiatsu training days, he has always been friendly and welcoming, as well as insightful. Since then I have attended training in Waveform Energetics and Remote Viewing with Mike and Stella, his wonderful wife. My life has definitely been enhanced by his teachings, and through spending time and communicating with both Mike and Stella.

Mike's first book was a good introduction to Waveform Energetics and energy, and also illustrated Mike's approach to working with energy awareness.

This second book builds on his previous book whilst also being able to be read and engaged with independently. The content is accessible and grounded with Mike's everyday life examples, as well as prompting the reader to look beyond what may be accepted as their reality, to realise the influence of 'programming' and its considerable impact on daily moment to moment life despite often being unconscious. There are links made to ancient and more modern teachings, giving even more richness to the text.

Mike emphasises the role of readiness, choice and commitment. Is now your time of readiness? Mike's book has many pearls which may facilitate you to go beyond your current life, perhaps to face your fears. You may choose to take the next steps on your own, with the support of Mike's book(s) and other resources, or access Waveform Energetics or other training.

As ever, Mike shares his life happenings in an honest and respectfully transparent way, helping the reader to understand that he himself has had significant life challenges. Hence his words are grounded in life, whilst also encouraging each reader to have the opportunity to go beyond.

Julie Tasker
BSc(Hons) BA(Hons) PGCE
Former Vice President of the Federation of Holistic Therapists
Health Kinesiology Practitioner and Tutor
The Healing Trust Practitioner and Tutor
Reiki Master Practitioner and Tutor

Introduction

This second slim book was started almost immediately after the completion of the first book, 'A Simple Guide to Voyaging the Energetic Universe'. Work interfered; trips abroad to teach also took their toll on creativity, rhythm and flow.

The new book took a back seat as continuous development in Waveform accelerated our insights and skills to new levels of awareness. Some of the realisations and lessons learned are included in this book.

This volume assumes that you have a conscious connection with the Energetic Universe and that you wish to continue your voyage to 'BE' and well as 'DO'.

The chapters within explore aspects of both, although the possibility of life after death is viewed from a Waveform experiential point of view with the emphasis on life, and living life supremely well.

We wish to bring to you the magic and excitement of the experiences that await you in the Energetic Universe. All that is available to you has always been available here and now. We do not have to go 'somewhere' to experience this magic; we travel through time and across distance silently, either un-noticed or making our presence felt every step of the way.

We must look deeper into ourselves as our power – yes, POWER – increases and we face and accept the dark side of ourselves. Our magic can be used for the greater good, not always visible as a Harry Potter flick of the wand, since real power lies in its hidden strength. The important subject of personal responsibility with growing awareness is emphasised here.

That the universe listens to us and acts on our subconscious desires has a direct effect on time and impact on the present. When we understand how this process works we realise the importance of creating a clear picture of the future we wish for. We also have to prepare ourselves to recognise the route to this goal created by the Universe, which may not be the one that we had envisaged.

Whilst the first book was mainly about developing skills within the Energetic Matrix, this book explores some of the implications of our developing relationship. The emphasis is more on 'being' than on 'doing'; of spiritual realisation and personal growth rather than enhancing our abilities as voyagers within the Energetic Matrix. The latter will, however, continue to expand in line with our growing understanding and awareness of the Universal environment and its full involvement in our daily lives.

As we continue to develop our relationship with the universe, it is transformed from a distant and impersonal energy force into that of a close and personal learned friend - wise in all things, a trusted confidante who is ready to teach you the secrets of the Universe.

As always, the prerequisite for receiving lessons from the universe is 'readiness', not keenness. When you are open and ready to take the next steps the universe will provide.

The chapters within this book may seem unconnected but each one explores how we may voyage more deeply into the matrix and realise our place in universal consciousness. Some chapters explain how to improve your level of readiness; others provide advice on surmounting the challenges that you may encounter on your journey.

Each of us is different, unique, therefore our voyage will present challenges and lessons created uniquely for us. What this book contains is information that prepares us for some of the common experiences and lessons awaiting us in the Energetic Matrix and, as your journey brings you into 'wholeness', you are also faced with the huge responsibility that 'wholeness' includes.

What will you do with your newly found power? Will it be used solely for your personal gain, or will it be used for the greater good?

Mike Webster. Loch Lomond. Scotland.

1

Mastery - A Continuous Process

'Mastery involves more than just the demonstration of competence in a particular skill. It also involves learning the rules and principles that underlie that particular skill and integrating these at both conscious and unconscious levels. In this way the rules and principles of the 'skill' are fully understood at the deepest level and are therefore demonstrated appropriately, and with ease in the face of continuously changing circumstances.'

True Mastery is a continuous process and not an end in itself. Each of us is an emergent Master as we tread the path to understanding and discern how to apply this in our daily lives. No-one is in a position to judge or has a right to judge our degree of spiritual 'mastery' because our journey in this life is but a tiny manifestation of Universal Consciousness, which is well beyond the comprehension of us mere mortals.

Mastery is not an accumulation of knowledge, but of wisdom which surpasses knowledge, being fully present in reality in the NOW.

'This is no magnificent deed, because I do not want followers, and I mean this. The moment you follow someone you cease to follow Truth.'

In 1929 in the Netherlands, Jiddu Krishnamurti gave a speech to several thousand people during which he announced that he was leaving the Order of the Star. He stated that did not want to be a Guru to be followed, because it meant that people would listen to him and follow him instead of looking inside themselves for the truth.

'Mastery' means Mastery of your path which is unique to you. Its routes and destination are part of the universal plan ready to be revealed to you as you voyage the universe, gaining wisdom from the challenges and experiences that are presented to you. It is THE journey of a lifetime.

2

THE INTELLIGENT, SELF-AWARE UNIVERSE

If you do a deal with the Universe along the lines of 'If you do this for me I will do that' make sure you keep your part of the bargain.

The title of this chapter is descriptive of my personal, direct experience. I can understand when people speak of having a personal relationship with God, as my experience is a similar one with the Universe.

As in all relationships promises are expected to be kept

I learned very early on that agreements with the Universe were meant to be honoured, and if such agreements included long-term plans, which the Universe has put into motion, changing your mind may not slow down or change what is already well under way.

The following story illustrates this point very well.

I loved my cottage, but it was time for change and I reluctantly accepted that the time had come to move to the populated area I had seen in my meditation. With a heavy heart I placed the cottage on the market; and as the final minutes towards the closing time for offers in the Scottish tradition ticked away, I had no idea as to where I was going to live, or what I was going to do.

At the appointed time I contacted my solicitor to find out what the highest bid was for my home, knowing that two people would be bidding around the price I had hoped for. It came as a shock to find that the higher bid (in fact the only one) had been withdrawn without explanation only minutes before the closing time. The solicitor was also puzzled as it was also a novel and strange experience for her.

Stunned, I returned home. What had gone wrong? Had the plans for me changed in some way and I had not recognised this? I telephoned Joy, my Orkney teacher.

Joy's response was: 'You changed your mind, didn't you!' This was followed with, 'You reneged on your deal with the Universe'.

I started to protest!

Joy continued: 'On the sale of the cottage, you had secretly decided to stay in Inverness despite having agreed with the Universe that you would move to a larger, more populated area like Glasgow; so you changed your mind.'

Digging deeply into my soul, I realised that my head and my heart did not have the same agenda. My head wanted to sell the cottage and move on. My heart wanted to stay in the Inverness area. So why was this?

During my last troubled year at St Martins I had met a wonderful soul. Friendship had developed into love, and my faith in myself and my self-esteem had started to return. In brief, life was worth living again.

Stella was not able to just drop everything and leave to be with me, but I could not bring myself to move away from her. This, as it was clearly pointed out to me, was not what had been agreed with the Universe. I realised that the cottage was not going to sell until it was clear to the Universe that I was going to honour my agreement.

The weeks that followed were agonising, but there was no room for compromise. I was either staying at St Martins, where I could still see Stella and have a continuation of spiralling debts, or I could sell St Martins, debts cleared, and negotiate a future in somewhere like Glasgow without Stella (as things presently stood).

One day, on the road between Culbokie and Cullicudden on the Black Isle, approaching what is known locally as the Cullicudden Straight, I stopped walking and shouted, 'Alright, I'll do it, I'll leave the area.'

I searched my heart for any holding back, and there was none – I had made up my mind. It was a further 20 minutes before I was back home at St Martins – the phone was ringing, it was my solicitor. The cottage had been sold!

Honour any bargain you have made with the Universe

Whilst we always have a choice and an opportunity for change, we must remain aware of whether what is changing is from a request for ourselves to the Universe, or whether we have struck a bargain with the Universe, and also how advanced the plans have become.

In my case my home was being sold for various reasons, one of which was so I could move south near Glasgow to be near a larger population to teach. I would also be near an international airport to take me to the many countries it had been predicted I would take Waveform to. Almost immediately after my move I was invited to teach in Switzerland. This was the start of many trips to different countries in Europe that have continued to this day.

That is what I mean when I say that if you do a deal with the Universe along the lines of 'If you do this for me I will do that' make sure you keep your part of the bargain.

The Universe as a teacher.

Often whilst teaching, I have moved outside of my scheduled work to make a point of some kind. It has always been to make the student perceive something beyond narrow self-imposed boundaries. Whilst I have been considering this, the Universe has taken the opportunity to step in and provide the ideal situation.

The Universe first of all sets a puzzle for me to work out, before I can create one for the student. What is provided by the Universe is always exactly what is needed for me and also the student(s).

My observations are that, immediately we step outside of our map of the Universe and limiting beliefs, the Universe steps in and teaches us, often with a dry sense of humour. When this happens I am reminded of the lessons I received in the Sanday group in Orkney.

The Universe has a sense of humour

My brief glimpses of clairvoyance often contained lessons that were humorous. My inflexibility of mind was depicted as a wooden toy soldier riding a wooden toy horse with little pencilled clouds of dust rising as we stiffly trotted along.

Lesson received and understood.

It was also a very accurate depiction of my riding skills. Here is another example.

Stella and I were visiting our good friends, Chris and Sue, who live near the Jodrell Bank telescope. The day Stella and I left for home, we started early so that we could visit the JB centre. It turned out to be too early and the centre was not yet open to visitors. The grounds, however, were open, we could smell newly cut grass and the sun was shining. We ventured over towards a grassed area with ponds and trees and bathed in the sunshine, while watching the dragonflies doing their stuff over the ponds which had the last vestiges of the morning mist.

I was waxing lyrical about the oneness of all things. Stella listened patiently. We settled beneath a beautiful beech tree resplendent in leafy green. I droned on and on, carried away with my own rhetoric. Then, something hit me on the head.

It was squirrel shit!

The Universe always has a way of pulling me up short when I get too intense – too 'spiritual' or I just need knocking down to earth again. This day was no exception and we couldn't stop laughing!

A Self-Aware Universe

That the Universe is self-aware is more difficult to demonstrate as it is subject to our personal experience.

If I were to personalise my experience of the Universe I would describe the Universe's responses and actions as those of someone who is self-aware - knowing when I have learned a lesson and providing another one when the timing was right.

This personal realisation that the universe is self-aware will come as no surprise to those that believe in a personal God. To those that believe in Universal Consciousness or Universal Mind there may be a subtle difference in understanding and perception of a self-aware Universe.

My personal experience is that at the roots there is no difference between the two viewpoints. It is all down to how it is packaged, presented and perceived: God – Universal Consciousness.

Once again our perception is governed by our programming, our culture and our personal maps of the world. Once we step outside of this self-imposed straitjacket, our direct personal experience is what makes our chosen path real to us and opens our minds to realising our connection to the Great Unknown.

3

ME-SELF-I

The Path to full understanding is revealed when the artificial 'self', which consists of our programming and preconceptions, intellectualisation and labelling, is stripped away. Here we are face to face with our original self and we perceive reality in full awareness.

Programming, labels, the intellect, beliefs, values, maps of the world, concepts constructed and shaped from birth all dictate how we view the world and those we share it with.

These 'add-ons' may be likened to the skins of an onion, the layers of which create a screen between us and reality. This screen clouds or obstructs our senses from what is really there and narrows our view of real life.

What we see is a constructed and artificial, individual view of the world. No-one else has your programming, your map but it is **your** reality not **the** reality that underpins everything and from which we have all emerged.

We are a multicultural society with diverse ethnic groups and of different skin colours. When all is stripped away we are, in essence, the same; our needs are the same: warmth, food, water, shelter, to love and be loved. It is at this core level that we realise that we are the same - human beings with basic needs. It is at this level that the artificial divisions - barriers based on our programming - dissolve in a common need and shared experience. There is unity in a common cause.

Being reborn each moment of our lives.

When we were born we only had the programming of the womb. This means our pre-birth conditioning - what we experienced in the womb - is the start of our conditioning. To be 'reborn' without any programming we have to go back before we were conceived – to our source, our true home.

To be 'reborn' each moment of our lives we can choose to shed all conditioning, the intellect, labels and preconceptions and in their place perceive the sounds, sensations - all input from the senses without thought.

In this moment become truly present and aware – your life will change.

According to Maslow identity is at the top of the pyramid of our neurological levels, the things that shape us and create our map of the world: Environment/Culture, Behaviour, Capabilities/Skills, Beliefs and Values, Identity.

Beyond Identity is our vision for the greater good - our spiritual aspirations.

Identity

Identity is what we perceive ourselves to 'be'.

As a young person we may express our identity by our clothing, who we mix with, where we are seen, what we do. Our yearning to 'belong' can be a symptom of our separation from the 'whole' and yet this sort of belonging is often temporary and we move onto another group that provides a new identify for us - for the time being.

As a mature individual, who and what we are can be clear on one level - retired teacher, engineer or pilot - but our inner identity remains elusive.

This inner sense of who we are may be shaped by a lifetime of programming or, by creating more time for self, we can start to see the world as we have never seen it before. The world and ourselves may appear as strangers and perhaps it is time to get acquainted with both – new world, new person = new reality.

For as long as we cling to the 'I', we carry with us programming that will slow us down as we explore the multidimensional Universe. Whilst we are occupied and over-identified with the 'I', we will not have a clear concept of the reality that lies before us, around us, within us.

We can start to remove the layers we have constructed within us and see the Universe as it really is.

4

ON LETTING GO!

> *Change **is** possible; it is a question of awareness. And once we change ourselves we change society and the world in which we find ourselves. Understanding ourselves is the beginning of wisdom.*

On reading this heading, one might understandably ask the question. 'What do I have to let go of and… why?' To answer this question let us start with 'Why?'

In 'A Simple Guide to Voyaging the Energetic Universe' (VEU) we discussed how personal programming narrows our focus and shapes our individual view of reality.

Addressing our programming to remove or update out-of-date programmes, and those which limit or impair our path through life, is a starting-point to seeing life as it really is. This 'letting go' of obsolete programmes that are no longer useful reveals a new perception of life.

What do I have to let go of?

The simple and most direct answer to this question is - everything!

This, however, is not a particularly helpful answer, so let us look specifically at what we 'let go' of and what 'letting go' actually means.

Letting go and vows of poverty.

Poverty is one of the vows taken by many living in monastic communities. However, in a more complete sense, 'poverty' may be seen as the state of mind lying behind the material condition, which itself is only an outward sign of 'poverty'.

The terms 'surrendering' and 'letting go' become more relevant when seen as unconditional requirements to enter a new state of perception. When there is trauma or mental chaos there is nothing for the mind to hold on to. When you perceive that you have nothing, have lost everything, there is nothing to lose and space is cleared and the way to a new perception is open to you. [1](Enlightenment? Not just now thank you!)

To acquire a new perception through trauma is not exactly a first choice for anyone, nor is giving away one's possessions in the hope that a state of 'material poverty' is sufficient for a door to open to a new perception.

If internal poverty or letting go has not already taken place before one gives everything away, hope and faith can be replaced by less desirable thoughts and feelings such as loss and uncertainty and even resentment, all of which may add to rather than remove obstacles from the mind.

We return once again to the outward representation of internal poverty or letting go. At best, internal and external poverty are congruent and letting go on both levels is a natural part of the process. At worst, the outer show of poverty is not a mirror of the inner state. This leaves a question mark as to the reasons for the pretence and the conflict between the inner and outer person.

'Poverty' suggests a lack of something and is therefore perhaps not the best choice of words to describe an inner state of freedom from attachment to possessions both material and mental.

This brings us to the third question. How can we let go?

The illusion of self

Unless we are fully aware of our connection with the Universe, which we can recognise by alignment of the conscious and unconscious minds, we operate each day of our lives from an artificial structure created by our internal programming which had been installed, and continuously updated since birth. Everything we do has a 'trigger' - something which stimulates a thought, a feeling or a physical action. If we analyse these responses in depth it might appear that we have little more free will than a machine. This is our programming at work which has shaped our individual maps and view of the world, from which we construct our own artificial view of reality.

Whilst we can address our programming and our alignment between head and heart (the conscious rational mind and the Universe) there are some simple things we can do on a daily basis which expose our everyday programming and we can choose whether to change or not. With understanding and soul-searching we do have a choice.

To know what to 'let go' of we first learn to accept our physical selves as we are; then our habits and programming that we are unaware of and rule us, pull our strings, govern our responses, create our map of the world.

Become an observer of self

To become an observer of self, the first requirement is to accept that all observations are made without any form of judgement. If the reader has read 'A Simple Guide to Voyaging the Energetic Universe', remember the chapter on Being Present and Aware.

Non-judgement starts with the simple task of observing one's own hands, in full concentration, perhaps truly seeing them for the very first time. Observe the lines, the colours, the marks and scars, the wrinkled skin – whatever is there. Just look, as though for the first time in your life.

These hands carry out a wide range of tasks. They are a major kinaesthetic link with the sensory world that is often taken completely for granted. These hands are yours to command. They touch your loved one with tenderness; they help to operate the controls of your car, keep you facing where you want to go; they collect wood, carry the shopping, prepare food, pull the covers over you at the end of the day.

Look at these hands with full attention as though they are someone else's hands; be fully present. Seen from a position of non-judgement, the scars, the cracked nails, the wrinkles are all a part of their reality, it is what they are – appreciate them. All of your body can be observed and appreciated in this way. It is your physical vehicle. Be grateful and appreciate it for what it is.

Observe your habits

Do you have a daily newspaper? What is it that you gain from reading this? Observe the topics, the stories that attract you. What do you gain from these?

Be honest and non-judgemental about how it is that you benefit from reading these papers on a daily basis. Is it an overview of what is happening in the world? If so, how do you respond to these events? Do you take action where you can? Do some events make you grateful for what you have? Do they bring a bit of excitement into your life?

Search your feelings for your response, be honest with yourself about how you feel but do not judge yourself.

If what you gain from the newspaper is essential to you there is no need to change since your reasons are relevant for you. If you feel that these reasons are not contributing to your values in life or for any other reason then leave the habit behind. Start stripping away what does not contribute to the quality of your life.

Observe your responses

There is a saying: there is a space between stimulus and response – use it wisely!

We respond to stimuli both verbal and mental many dozens of times a day, every day of our lives. Our senses are trained to respond from birth.

We are conditioned and trained by our parents, our siblings and all who we come in contact with from an early age to respond to stimuli in certain ways. Children may respond to their parents' refusal to give them another ice cream by screaming and, if that does not work, by screaming louder until the parents give in just because it is the easiest thing to do and to have some peace and quiet - stimulus and response on both sides. The teenager may continue to press a request for a new cell phone, producing new arguments until the parents, with less stamina than the teenager, give in.

The child who moved into adulthood unable to express a deep need - because 'children should be seen and not heard' - may believe that they are unworthy of attention. Then there are responses such as 'taking offence' when someone disagrees with what someone has else has said or doesn't like hearing, which may even be the truth. Those who are on the defensive feel the need to protect themselves if a simple and harmless question is asked of them that they don't wish to answer. Other responses to unwelcome questions may provoke a personal attack on the questioner.

On an international level we see this game played out, as leaders of one nation respond violently, at great cost to human life, to what they consider to be a threat (real or imagined) by another nation.

Often the threat is not backed by evidence but is considered 'obvious' and concrete because it suits their purpose and they are seen to be 'doing something' about it.

Alone, we may not be able to change the world but we can change ourselves for the greater good and have the tools to do this.

One subtle but damaging response is to look for hidden meaning behind someone's words and then act as if your guesswork is the truth of that matter. This is a good place to start the process of changing your responses.

Do you recognise this situation?

Teenager or adult says, 'I am hungry'.

Parent/partner gets up from what they are doing and gets them something to eat.

The response to the statement was to guess the message behind the words. This response was acceptable before the child had speech and the parent had to guess what the crying meant, but is inexcusable from anyone who has the power of speech.

The child has not learned to take responsibility in asking for something to eat and the parent has continued their pattern of guessing what message lies behind the words. Unless corrected, this pattern can carry on through childhood into adulthood. Communication then becomes a matter of guesswork.

'Taking offence' can easily become an undesirable, automatic response

Vagueness and guesswork lead to the creation of undesirable responses, suspicion, defensiveness, misunderstandings and we find offence where none was intended. We take offence, stand up for ourselves, we feel attacked, put down, we feel we must retaliate. We create a response to scenarios that exist only in our minds. Even our judgements about who and what we are, good or bad, right or wrong are creations from our programming.

We are puppets of our programming, responding by force of habit or our fertile minds, so listen to what you hear – use the space between stimulus and response wisely.

What does our subconscious mind feel about how we respond and what do we truly no longer need in our lives? What can we let go of that frees us just a little bit more from the tunes we dance to that are unwittingly created by ourselves? Does that remark that we would normally respond to angrily, because it is a part of our habit pattern, really matter - deep down, does it really matter? Do we really feel offended or is it just that we have got used to responding in this way?

Do we realise that our responses, our patterns have absolutely nothing to do with what we really are, and are an artificial creation that we play out on a daily basis?

When we take all this away we are left with the real being we do not recognise: the being that is unhindered by programming and sees life as it really is, non-judgementally and with clarity.

Here at last is the truth we have been seeking, and it was always there before our eyes.

This chapter has been a long one compared to the others and, whilst the phrase 'Letting go' contains all the information, the Why and the How **are** explained in this chapter and others that follow.

The secret to success works not by presenting a fake copy to the world of what you would like the inner state to be but by creating authentically from the inside, and showing to the world your external face which is a reflection of your internal state.

Letting go from the inside is true liberation.

To Recap

Material and mental possessions in themselves are not a problem, except that attachments to them obscures reality from our external and internal vision and experience – the reality of who or what we are and our intimate connection with life.

Think of our programming, our map of the world, our possessions, material and mental, like the skins of an onion. Strip them away and at the centre there is nothing. In our case there is the essence of what we are and a direct connection with life that is obscured by layers of something that does not exist. It is we that give it substance and life.

Once we have challenged our responses and removed from our lives the habits that no longer serve us we have come to the step that Huang Po (9th Century Buddhist Chan Master) urged his followers to take.

Remove all labels and concepts, intellectualisation, and judgements and you will be faced with reality. At this point, the Universe opens up to you. Again, the most important requirement is 'Readiness'.

*Change **is** possible; it is a question of awareness. And once we change ourselves we change society and the world in which we find ourselves. Understanding ourselves is the beginning of wisdom.*

5

Enlightenment – Whatever that means to you!

Whether sudden and complete or incremental, the key state is 'Readiness'. When you are ready the shift takes place. The change may be seamless; one moment there is relative blindness and the next clarity and realisation.

We are told by the 'great ones', the Roshis, the Lamas, masters of many routes to Enlightenment that we are already 'Enlightened' but most of us don't know it. That it is merely a case of being totally present and fully aware, fully awake to make this change in perception. This opportunity we are told we can take at any moment in time, even right now!

Why is it that with so much of the world seeking union with God, Enlightenment etc. so few gain that intuitive understanding and profound realisation, which in Buddhist terms is known as Enlightenment?

Paradoxically, when the greater majority of those that have conscientiously sought Enlightenment for most of their lives die without having this profound realisation, the major leaps in awareness and changes in perception of life actually arise during times of trauma and mental chaos.

From my own experience I believe that we are all presented with a number of opportunities in life to make this realisation, and are not aware enough to recognise them as such.

Michael, a friend and colleague told me recently about his experience with a Buddhist Roshi who was advising a group that they could be 'enlightened' within a year, a month, a week an hour or right now if that was what they really wanted. Michael said that there was silence, and a lot of 'shuffling of feet'. So what was the problem, where were the willing volunteers?

Michael's story reminded me of my own experiences. At least twice in my life I have known without doubt what life was about, and lost it all in a flash as my analytical mind kicked in.

More recently however, sitting quietly in my garden, on two different occasions I experienced the door of realisation opening and I had only to take a step forward to experience and understand what I had searched for all of my life.

I pulled back, and the 'door' closed again.

Why did I pull back? In front of me was what I had wanted in life for as long as I could remember? The answer was – fear! [1] Ref article in appendix.

Creating a State of Readiness.

There are many ways to create a state of readiness; one method which is taught in Waveform Post Graduate workshops provides a structured means of stripping away the labels and concepts that get in the way of a new perception of life. Although this method can be carried out on one's own, it requires one to be fully present and aware along with discipline and an awareness of what is happening as the process progresses. It also requires a recognition of emotions as they arise and the ability to recognise and return to the stage one had reached. We encourage Waveform graduates who are practised and experienced in working with Emotional Resonances to work together in pairs and coach each other through what arises as the process progresses.

This is the most effective way of carrying out this exercise as the coach makes the active participant dig deeper, stripping away more descriptions and labels. In this way the participant does not have to multitask i.e. follow the stripping away with the self-evaluation of 'How do I feel?'

In front of you is the gate to Enlightenment, everything you see has the potential to open the gate for you, you just need to know HOW.

You can carry out this process with any object you like. Everything contains the key to a new perception of life. My advice is not to select anything that you find highly emotive. This will create an added challenge in the process - something else to get in the way.

The principle is to remove the labels without destroying what the object is. The skill of the coach is to be able to challenge, and to keep challenging the answers the seeker provides.

There is a point when the intellect is unable to find an answer. At this point the seeker may hit what we call 'the wall', having used up their labels and descriptions for the moment. It is a time of uncertainty when the intellect has ground to a temporary halt. An emotion is then transmitted.

The coach feels the emotion that has been transmitted and challenges the seeker:

'What is it that you are feeling?'

The seeker addresses the meaning of the emotion e.g. 'fear'.

'What is it that you are fearful of?'

The matter is explored and the cause of the fear is identified. At this point the seeker may rationalise the fear.

'What am I afraid of?'

'The unknown?'

'Changes in my life?'
Whatever it is I have a choice.

a) To stop the process of forward movement in the exercise.
b) To accept and rationalise the fear and move forward again.

A break may be desirable to explore the emotion and make a choice to stop or move forward again. The coach may assist the seeker in exploring their choices, once they have found out what they are.

This may take the form of an NLP 'Parts Management' exercise or other decision- making processes that explore the subconscious mind, followed by a reality check of the choices made.

If the seeker chooses to stop the process there may be a realisation that they made a choice of their own free will – and so it really was not a question that the 'Gods had not smiled on them'.

If the seeker chooses to move forward the process is renewed. A fresh start is made with the same object and quickly they arrive at the same place where they stopped before.

a) If the emotion arises again, they can once more explore it.
b) If the way is clear emotionally the seeker is now freed of the emotion and searching for another label to strip away.
c) Moving forward, another emotional wall is detected
d) Exploring and deciding takes place once again.

The seeker will be aware that their 'salvation' is in their own hands. They **choose** to remove themselves from the process. Insight may be gained, however, at each hitting of the wall.

1) Readiness? Not ready
2) Accepting fear of change. Ready.
3) Happy where they are for the time being.
4) Faced with the Void

Profound Realisation, Sudden or Incremental?

Process and personal development realisations can be sudden or incremental.

Think of St Paul's epiphany on the road to Damascus, the Buddha's Enlightenment or the sudden, personal and profound realisations of perhaps many thousands of people over the centuries. Soto Zen emphasises sudden realisation by the use of riddles (koans) that by-pass the rational mind. And there are other methods that take longer, based on meditation. Each of us in our daily lives has the opportunity to have experiences of realisation, expanding awareness and understanding, whether incrementally, in small realisations or through a sudden leap in awareness and understanding which takes place in a fraction of a second.

Whether sudden and complete or incremental, the key preparatory state is 'Readiness'. When you are ready the shift takes place. The change may be seamless; one moment there is relative blindness and the next, clarity and realisation. There may also be a transitional phase, chaos as the bits drop into place. A mounting realisation like a build-up to a sneeze or when you find yourself faced with what is known as The Void.

When you are confronted with The Void you are completely on your own.

STEPPING INTO THE VOID

Ordinary people look to their surroundings, while followers of the Way look to Mind, but the true Dharma is to forget them both. The former is easy enough, the latter very difficult. Men are afraid to forget their minds, fearing to fall through the Void with nothing to stay their fall. They do not know that the Void is not really void, but the realm of the real Dharma.

Finally we reach the stage which is often called The Void.

In everything, including matters spiritual, we have choice.

What is The Void? It is not a place in the sense of something that exists, that waits for us to arrive and walk into. It is a place or more accurately a 'state' of transition that we create for ourselves when the time and conditions are right for it to manifest. It is another example of 'Readiness'!

This place is devoid of labels, intellectualisation, judgements, concepts, even the concept of 'self'. My own experience of The Void was of a place with nothing to hold onto mentally or otherwise. A place where all of what was 'me' had gone except my fear of what I could not control, this place in which I was stripped of everything including self, my existence.

My experiences of The Void taught me a very valuable lesson.

In everything including matters spiritual we have choice. Even as the Universe takes the last step for us we have choice. That power of choice enables us to make decisions for ourselves; we may become both empowered and enlightened with a fuller understanding of our final steps which formerly we perhaps believed could be taken only by the grace granted by a higher authority.

This realisation takes away the belief that, compared to what we already have, there is something better awaiting us, and we realise that what we already have is a part of our Universal wholeness. We do not pass to a different place only to have a different perception of what is already there.

My experiences of The Void confirmed for me my contentment with my life and with whom I share it.

When finding yourself in The Void for the first time - as if in a whirlpool with no escape - your fear may pull you back. The second time you experience The Void you recognise your response and, on returning to the world of self, labels and concepts, you have the opportunity to evaluate your experience: why the fear, what was I fearful of?

My own experiences were a huge step forward in the realisation that I had made a choice, I could have gone with The Void and surrendered to it but I chose to step back.

My realisation was that I was content with my life and my fear was about losing what I was content with.

As always in things energetic and spiritual, the state that facilitates change is 'Readiness'. I was not ready then and I am still not ready to take this final step.

If I had surrendered to The Void how might I change as a person? Would the 'new me' change my relationship with my wife? How different would I appear to her and would I still be what she wanted which was the present me, with all my human foibles and faults?

Imperfect as I am, she loves me for what I am. I could not take the risk of changing that because beyond The Void there is no going back.

The Void is a place of transition.

A route to The Void is provided in the previous chapter and is an application of the time-honoured advice given by Huang Po and others who have trodden the path to their own profound realisations: remove all labels and concepts, mind-chattering and intellectualisation and you will find yourself at the door of clarity and full understanding of life and your place in the Universe.

At some point along the path you will find yourself in The Void. There is no warning - you are just there. Remember it is a place of transition and not a permanent state. Our experience will be unique as The Void is our own creation which manifests at the point of readiness.

Your fears are based on uncertainty, finding yourself facing the unknown, feelings of nothing to hold onto, nothing to hold on with. Disorientation like waking up in the middle of the night and not knowing where you are - nothing is familiar to you.

There is really nothing to fear but your fear, and you have choice: to surrender and go forward, or to turn back. Whichever you chose will be the right decision for you at this time.

Now that you have a means to approach the point of transition - The Void - you can prepare for the journey. Readiness is the key word throughout the process and commitment is required providing the momentum to get you through and out the other side. It may be that once under way, having challenged your experiences of 'hitting the wall', you may still not be ready for the final step. Accept that you are not ready but make sure that you understand the reasons for this choice. My reasons are clear to me and, knowing what they are, I do not have any feelings of having missed out in any way.

The Void is only one of a number of transformational phases or steps. Some of these are immediate such as my own at the age of 26, and again on the Isle of Bute aged 53. There have been other profound experiences where realisation took place after a process in my mind made connections like building blocks being rapidly assembled, or as in the example of the build-up to a sneeze. Realisation and understanding took place at the apex of the process which, from start to finish, took no more than a couple of seconds.

Each of these precious moments provides a priceless gift of clarity and understanding. Take time to be fully present and aware and you will recognise these opportunities as they arise for you.

The universe gives you choices; only man tells you that 'My way is The Way'.

No! **My** way is the way'.

The reality is that YOUR way is THE way. Your path is the only reality for you.

7

ORDINARY AND ENLIGHTENED.

What is life?
It is the flash of a firefly in the night.
It is the breath of a buffalo in the wintertime.
It is the little shadow which runs across
the grass and loses itself in the sunset.

Several months ago I received a phone call from a woman who was interested in participating in our basic Waveform course. She asked me what Waveform was and during the course of the conversation she asked me if I had ever met anyone who was 'enlightened'.

I spoke about my friend, the Orkney farmer, who had a deep natural understanding of life, his farm, his animals and the seasons - a state of mind, which to him was completely natural. He was amongst the most enlightened people I have ever met.

Moments later the woman asked me the same question again. This ordinary unknown farmer could not possibly be 'enlightened'; he just did not fit into the mould! Unknown, not religiously trained or even inclined, he did not meditate or do Yoga, Tai Chi or wear the right clothing. He just did not fit the image of an enlightened person as perceived through her map of the world.

My experience is that the vast majority of seekers consider 'enlightened' persons in much the same way.

I did not add to my description of Michael that he drank whisky, killed and ate his own animals, the latter being carried out in full consciousness of the animal's sacrifice, with responsibility and appreciation of life. No! Michael did not fit into the stereotype of an enlightened person and yet his ordinary, everyday life was congruent, sincere, honest and shone with truth. Not that these words would have meant anything to Michael - this was just his life and the way he lived.

Treat everyone as though they are 'Enlightened'.

If we live in a busy place we could be passing an enlightened person many times a week. A person may be enlightened and unaware of the fact that their perception of life and the Universe is not the same as the greater majority of the people on this planet; or it could be a person who chooses to live a simple life uncluttered by modern technology or the trappings of the consumer society. Their behaviour may be considered odd, eccentric even. It may be that they have all they want and are content with their simple life.

When one reads the words of some of the first peoples of North America one cannot miss their deep connection with the land, life and their environment.

We do not know how far along the path any individual is on their spiritual journey and we have no right to judge. Someone we meet may not fit the criteria of what our map of the world considers an enlightened person to be. That, however, is a limitation created by our map of the world, our programming and also possibly our culture.

Enlightened people can wear the clothing of the farmyard, a loincloth or a business suit, for it is not what they wear that distinguishes them from everyone else. They may not have the language or the phrases that stick in people's minds. They may have a simplicity of speech and view of the world which, if taken superficially, can imply a lack of education or naivety because they do not have the appearance of an 'enlightened' person. They do not fit the stereotype we have become used to.

So that we do not grossly underestimate the people who enter our lives we may treat everyone as though they are 'Enlightened'.

8

MANIFESTING THE MIRROR

In the same way that internal change is reflected externally in your quality of life, the Universe is reflecting your internal state back to you.

At a certain level of awareness and alignment, the Universe responds overtly to your conscious requests and wishes, so be careful and mindful of what you wish for. The process of eliminating thoughts and habits that are no longer of use to you will reduce unwanted output, particularly those thoughts and higher feelings connected to the subconscious that the Universe listens and responds to. Personal alignment creates a direct and conscious connection with the Universe.

'Positive thinking' alone will not create the changes you want, no matter how hard you work at it. If your thinking and wishes are not aligned with the Universal aspect of your subconscious mind there is conflict between head and heart and so at best nothing happens or at worst there is despondency at the lack of results.

Looking in the mirror and saying, 'I am a good looking, intelligent human being whom everyone one wants to be with,' will not change what is looking back at you from the mirror and how you feel about yourself. The mirror is reflecting your inner state, how you truly feel about yourself.

The Universal mirror is also reflecting your inner state so be fully aware of what you are transmitting from your subconscious – being aligned makes this much easier.

Be mindful of your responses - they have power

Creating the change about how you feel about yourself takes place from within, from the subconscious mind, not from the conscious mind. If there is conflict between head and heart, create a discussion between them as described in 'Voyaging the Energetic Universe' (VEU). Come to an agreement between them and move forward only when you have this agreement.

The Universe will then listen to you and act on your wishes, locally as well as universally.

It is the grasshopper mind of the human that creates confusion along the path he/she walks.

Be mindful of your responses (see chapter on Letting Go); they have power, and once the signal is sent 'on your instructions' they have effect. Mostly the effect of the signal is filtered out by the receiver but some effect will have taken place. Your own filters will also have prevented you from realising that, in creating the signal, you mirror the effect in yourself.

Once you have the full realisation and personal experience of this effect, your life changes and you have massive responsibilities. You are now both cause and effect.

What you do to others you are now fully aware that you also do to yourself. The process of stripping away has revealed much that was hidden before. Moreover now you have the realisation that what you create in yourself is not only transmitted by the Universe to the target but is fully retained, unfiltered on a conscious level within yourself.

You feel what it is like to receive another's anger - only **you** are the sender of that anger. You feel the love that you have sent to another as though it was sent to you.

You are both sender/transmitter and receiver of that love.

How do you choose to act?

In developing levels of awareness there is also growing responsibility

The process of stripping away will have removed much of what you were not aware of and no longer need. It will have exposed those habits, thought processes and actions that do not enhance your life. You now have the means of enhancing your life by enhancing the lives of others. By giving you receive.

I recently came across this saying that bearing a grudge was like 'taking poison and expecting someone else to die from it'. There is a dark humour here which expresses very clearly the reality. Once we are aligned and conscious of our thoughts and feelings, brought to the surface by the process of stripping away, the truth is crystal clear.

With realisation and the awareness skills of fingerprinting and personal alignment one can transmit feelings to anyone across any distance.

This level of awareness and energy work has two sides. One can create love, confidence and feelings of self-esteem in anyone; but there is a darker side where one can create the opposite which manifests and lingers like a disease in its creator.

This level of energetic mastery and awareness is not taught in class but is available to those who will accept this level of responsibility for the greater good of all living things.

9

THE ENIGMA OF TIME

'Until one is committed, there is hesitancy, the chance to draw back, always ineffectiveness. Concerning all acts of initiative (and creation), there is one elementary truth the ignorance of which kills countless ideas and splendid plans: that the moment one definitely commits oneself, then providence moves too.

All sorts of things occur to help one that would never otherwise have occurred. A whole stream of events issues from the decision, raising in one's favour all manner of unforeseen incidents and meetings and material assistance, which no man could have dreamed would have come his way. Whatever you can do or dream you can do, begin it. Boldness has genius, power and magic in it.'

In 'A Simple Guide to Voyaging the Energetic Universe' we touched on how our heart communicates directly with the Universe and how personal alignment enables us to be completely aware of the messages/requests that we transmit to the Universe.

Clarity, commitment and flexibility are the key words to making the changes that you desire actually happen. I will also add another word here: 'timing'.

Whether we realise it or not, a single event scheduled for the future has an immediate effect on the energetic field. Globally the effect of your 'event' is minute but locally the effect is large and influences the lives of many (directly or indirectly) who are completely oblivious of their involvement in your scheduled 'event'. In order for this event to happen much will have to start to change 'now'. The whole process is not instantaneous and so requires time, creating new avenues and events to enable the desired event to materialise.

Think of it along the lines of a wedding. Two people decide to get married. A date is fixed; a place is selected; guests are chosen and invitations sent. The lives affected by this one event are far more than the bride and groom and all who are attending the wedding. Each small interaction creates a change in the lives of those indirectly involved whether florists, jewellers, or involved in transport, accommodation etc. Each interaction creates a change in whomsoever comes into contact with these people, and so on and so forth. There is a massive ripple effect from this one planned event. Some quickly peter out; others, reinforced, continue on their way. This ripple effect interacts with other newly created and also long-standing ripples, changing lives, directions and outcomes.

The start of the ripple of change is created by the future event.

Up until the decision to get married and the selection of date and venue a previous schedule of events and time will have been in place, operating in the present time. A new avenue of flow is now required, involving a subtle changing of events largely on a local time event continuum but with some influence on a planetary/Universal continuum.

Our lives are largely manipulated and directed by events; some are subtle and some not so subtle, as the Universe responds to the heartfelt wishes of others and events that have gathered momentum and are, as such, virtually unstoppable.

So let us look again at those four key words.

Clarity creates a picture of what we desire and endows it with colours, sounds, smells, form, feelings and movement.

Commitment creates the means to achieve this and will have laid in date and time the first practical steps towards this event taking place.

Flexibility allows us to be aware of the unexpected which may ultimately turn out to be a better route or event.

Timing is needed for the process of change to manifest in an effective or even transformational way; each event within the process takes place optimally within a narrow window of place and time. The Universe will calculate this for you and also plan the route that you take.

A large degree of patience and awareness is required while events are undergoing change in the present time. Much of what you are 'doing' seems to be slowing down or not happening at all. This is the time to broaden your focus - expand your awareness (FOR) and be ready for what is materialising.

These are critical and also exciting times for there is no straight line between you and the event you desire. It is not a question of life carrying on as usual as millions of small changes are taking place in the lives of others to enable your event to happen. Decisions for the future which are carried out with clarity, commitment, and flexibility will change events in the present time. We will not always be aware of what those 'changes' will be or when they will take place. Any small change, even by a second or two in the lives of others as a result of your future event, may present an experience that will change the course of a life. Where possible, take responsibility for this. There will be a time that is right to take certain actions with regard to your event, be aware and open to them manifesting and act appropriately. Timing!

In order for your future event to take place, events starting in the present will begin to change. The 'local' universe will make such changes as are required in order for this to happen and the changes may be the opposite of what you require in the present.

This brings us to some important points:

1) Be quite clear about what you want to happen.
2) Accept that a number of things will change as a result of this decision. The changes that take place will be more obvious on a local level and it may appear as though what 'normally' happens suddenly isn't happening as the process of movement closes down some processes and creates new ones more in keeping with the new event. This process takes time and what 'isn't' happening is more in evidence than what 'is' happening. Don't panic!
3) If, however, you are not aligned or aware of the messages that you are transmitting from your subconscious to the Universe, you may find yourself experiencing confusion with what is happening in your life as well as a feeling of lack of control over what happens to you, a victim of circumstance.

As clarity and commitment are missing from your subconscious, you are creating random transmissions which are not sustainable and you become more directed by life than directing, steered by ripples created by others' future events. Being fully present and aware allows you to fully participate in the unfolding of the Universal plan as it manifests on a local level. If the Universal plan conflicts with your local event, you will become aware of this very early on. Time to be flexible.

Timing is all important

In this chapter we have been faced once again with the power of focus and clarity and - more importantly - being fully present and aware. Be focussed but keep your options open and be flexible as this enables us to recognise and act upon unforeseen opportunities that the Universe provides.

This amazing truth was clearly demonstrated in Jenny's decision to leave London and search for a house near Joy, who had a home on the Black Isle near Inverness.

Here is Jenny's Story:

A house was found in Cromarty which seemed perfect for Jenny, and she was encouraged by Joy to go for it. However, some complications prevented the sale and Jenny was once again looking for a house. Jenny was unhappy about what had happened, particularly as other people were making comments about Joy, and that she had got it wrong about the house because the sale had fallen through.

What had happened?

I remembered my own experience of buying a house in the Inverness area and, after looking around for about a year and putting in a number of bids, we ended up exactly where Joy said we would be - on the Black Isle. However, until this particular time the cottage had not been for sale.

I pointed out to Jenny what I had learned that, as soon as she had made a clear and definite move towards what she wanted, she created changes in energy that have a ripple effect, and in turn bring about yet more changes. Everything then reorganises itself anew.

She may have lost the house that she wanted, but I suggested that she stand back and look again as more opportunities emerged from the knock-on effect and the changes that had taken place.

A house was found not more than 100 metres from Joy's home which was exactly what Jenny was looking for and formed a perfect base for the start of her new life.

This house had not been on the market when Jenny was looking for the ideal one to be near Joy. This was about timing, and also acceptance that the Universe has started the ripple effect which may not unfold as you think that it should. Step back and see what is manifesting. That something better is unfolding for you is often the case. Trust and be aware.

10

BI-LOCATION – SOMEWHERE IN TIME?

Bi-location, or sometimes multi-location, is an alleged psychic or miraculous ability wherein an individual or object is located (or appears to be located) in two distinct places at the same time.

Bi-location is usually simply described as the appearance of an individual in two places at once. There have been many famous cases of bi-location, particularly by mystics and saints, people such as Padre Pio of Italy who bore the stigmata of Christ. But is bi-location just a phenomenon that can only be carried out by highly evolved beings, and can it be only carried out by a deliberate act of will? My experience is that the answer to both of these questions is No!

In the 90's I awoke to the sound of a voice, and opened my eyes to see the face of my ex-mother-in-law in front of me. The disembodied voice said 'V***s mother is dead'.

I was informed of her death exactly a week later, and she had died on exactly the day and at the time the apparition had appeared. Whilst this may seem like an opener for a series of mother-in-law jokes, the experience was quiet and serene and the announcement was made in a matter of fact voice. Mother-in-law looked at me but didn't speak – which in my experience was unusual to say the least! It is true we didn't get on very well, so from all the people she could have chosen why did she appear to me? Was this a choice or an accident of some kind?

Four of our colleagues have contacted Stella and me in recent years to tell us that we have been visually present at either a healing or at a time of pain and stress. However, before anyone accuses us of setting ourselves on the same level as people such as Padre Pio, let me say that it was claimed by followers of Aleister Crowley, also known as 'The Great Beast', that he also bi-located. However, the only other thing that we have in common with Aleister Crowley that we are aware of is that neither he nor we were aware of the act of bi-locating!

As a Remote Viewer, my experience of what is classed by Remote Viewers as 'bi-location' is quite different from the usual definition in that the Remote Viewer is usually (if only vaguely) aware of where they physically are at the present moment, as well as where they are in space and time where their presence is not normally observed or even suspected.

The experience is similar to that of Waveform 'finger printers' (see 'The Vanishing Wizard' Positive Health on line Issue 172). When our fingerprinters (FP) are 'remotely' with the client, however, they can sometimes sense not only the presence of another fingerprinter but even who it may be, as each of us is constantly transmitting a unique identifiable signal.

When Waveform FPs are remotely with the client the interesting fact is that, wherever the client is located physically on the planet, to the 'finger printer' the location for them both is HERE and NOW.

Bi-location Across Time

In 2002 Stella and I decided to visit the people who now lived in my first croft of Little Isegarth on the Island of Sanday in the Orkney Islands.

This is my record of that event.

'We were made very welcome in the home that once was mine. It had been renovated and extended, and what had been outbuildings used for our animals and hay was now part of the house. I was pleased to see that after 20 plus years some of my handiwork was still intact in and around the garden and dykes (dry stone walls), which I had spent so much time creating and building. We had seen around the house without too much emotion as memories flitted in and out, and that was all that happened until we went back into the kitchen.

I gazed out of the kitchen window onto a view I had seen many hundreds of times before across the small front garden to the dyke I had built. Beyond the dyke was the small front field which stretched down to the road and the tidal flat from which Little Isegarth got its name. In the distance to the right the pier at Kettletoft could be seen, and to the left the land of Elseness, home of our friends the Seatters.

As I looked out on this so familiar scene my mind started to drift. The boundaries of past and present became fuzzy. Had the kitchen shifted back to the way I remembered it, or was this all in my mind? It was as though a distant memory was forming and becoming reality. Could I really hear the chickens in the garden? Was I really slipping back more than 20 years? The feeling was like being on the border between sleeping and waking, and I suddenly realised that the past was becoming more real with each second and the present was fading.

With effort I shook off my semi-sleep state and the 'present' returned. Fear had brought me back to my senses. I did not want to go back and relive the past again.

I turned and looked at Stella. For us life was good and I wanted to remain and live in the present.'

Was time such a fluid concept that its borders are permeable and we can move between different aspects of time - that is, if we allow ourselves and if the conditions are right?

In those few moments in Little Isegarth, looking out at the view I knew so well, it was as though the past was coming back into focus whilst the present became blurred, and started to dissolve the events of 20 years - taking Stella with it. Only fear of loss had stopped me from disappearing back into the past, to be relived again it seems. Only I feel that I would not have known it was the past.

Is what we see now as the present a re-treading of the past from a future no longer remembered?

Do I think that anyone can bi-locate or observe someone who has bi-located? My answer is – Yes!

In Waveform as in Remote Viewing the 'conscious' bi-locator follows a transmitted signal and arrives at the destination. The location of the transmitter of the signal is not always predictably in the present time. A signal could also be transmitting from the past or from the future, although this phenomenon happens more often with Remote Viewing than Waveform FP where the subject, to some degree, is a known factor.

'Is what we see now as the present a re-treading of the past from a future no longer remembered?'

What about the 'unconscious' bi-locator?

One description of the appearance and behaviour of a bi-locator suggests:

'Usually this 'double' acts strangely and mechanically, and does not acknowledge others when spoken to.' This to me does not sound like someone who has by an act of will appeared to someone else, but more the actions of someone who has no idea where they are, or what they are doing there!

So what brought them there?

My belief is that they are conveyed there in response to a transmitted signal, in the same way as a Remote Viewer and Waveform FP identify and consciously follow a transmitted signal.

Where does the signal come from?

I believe that the signal comes from the observer of the bi-locator, and may be the end-result of a mixture of conditions which give rise to a transmission. This transmission creates a signal line to a receptive 'address' from which there is an automated response.

This is not as far-fetched as it sounds when we consider another similar and familiar phenomenon. A child is away from home and has an accident and is frightened or is in danger . The child unknowingly sends out a 'signal' which mother (receptive address) picks up; instantly she recognises the transmitter of the signal (child) and acts on this information, either telephoning the child or driving to where the child is.

My experience in the fields of both Waveform and Remote Viewing is that, whether transmitting or receiving, emotions play a huge part as carriers of information - and we are transmitting information all of the time. Emotions penetrate levels of awareness like an alarm clock going off when you are asleep.

Most (but not all) reports of observed bi-location seem to be in situations of high emotion or anxiety, pain or despair - all high energy signals, mostly responded to in cases of bi-location by someone already familiar with, if not personally known to, the observer.

Bi-location is a response to a signal that has been transmitted, whether knowingly or unknowingly (by a person, or set of circumstances) and picked up by a 'receptive' receiver - another person who, it seems, can be either dead or alive, and who sends an automated reply back down the signal line i.e. they bi-locate.

My feeling is that not all cases of bi-location are visual.

We have other senses that recognise a unique signal, such as the smell of tobacco, or perfume of someone we know. We recognise the touch of a loved one; in our grief we sense the comforting presence and reassurance from someone, a 'receptive' address, now responding from another dimension - 'message received, all is well'.

'Fingerprinting' enables us to recognise individual energy fields, once connected transmissions are received and recognised. We may send a response to this transmission automatically and, depending on the strength of the signal received, bi-locate in response to a call for help, which is transmitted from the sender's subconscious mind. It would appear that we can consciously bi-locate, and that our subconscious mind responds (in our absence) to another's subconsciously transmitted requests for help by bi-locating to the site.

We will be aware of the former but not necessarily the latter. Our contact with the Universe through our subconscious mind has deemed the transmitted signal for 'help' of sufficient strength for us to respond in person. I have no doubts that the process is far from uncommon but few people are prepared to talk about it for fear of ridicule. The case of the mother who knows her child is in danger is a simple example of a transmitted signal from a known transmitter (the child) to a receiver that is open and receptive (the mother).

This brings me back to the fact that we are constantly transmitting and receiving information whether we realise it or not. That information is 'decoded' into thoughts, feelings and visual images. Our ability to receive, and how we receive the information, is governed by the strength of the signal, our knowledge of the transmitting fingerprint, our presence and awareness, our degree of alignment and our connection to the Universe.

11

Through the Veil of Death

I am the daughter of Earth and Water,
    And the nursling of the Sky;
I pass through the pores of the ocean and shores;
    I change, but I cannot die.
For after the rain when with never a stain
    The pavilion of Heaven is bare,
And the winds and sunbeams with their convex gleams
    Build up the blue dome of air,
I silently laugh at my own cenotaph,
    And out of the caverns of rain,
Like a child from the womb, like a ghost from the tomb,
    I arise and unbuild it again.

We Cannot Die

My experience suggests that death is only a transitional move into another dimension of functioning. Our experience of what exactly lies beyond the perceived barrier of death is limited but we can make contact and can communicate with the unchanging 'fundamental' facet the lies at the centre of each energetic being - the individual essence of that being that is detectable in life as we know it, and in the dimension we call death. The first step in this process is to identify the fundamental facet from the other facets that make up the individual fingerprint. We then have the energetic link between life and death and a door opens between these two dimensions.

Our early days of fingerprinting as an awareness technique provided us with clues as to what may be happening when a person neared death. Briefly we lost their 'fingerprint' (the unique part of a person's energy field that enables us to identify them wherever they are, no matter what time may have passed since we were last in contact with them).

We are often asked to provide Waveform alerts for our members to access those frequencies which are unique to any individual; and then make the changes the body mind requests. Usually we have no information other than the person's name and yet reports claim we are able to make changes in their condition that are noticeable and significant.

Our Waveform alerts come from all over the world; rarely do they come from immediate family, but usually from someone involved with Waveform, who knows of someone else who needs and has requested our help. All we need is the information that will help us to identify that person's unique 'fingerprint', ideally their name, where they are, what has happened to them and a photo, if possible. Rarely do we have all of this information and yet, with the information that we are given, we are still able to identify the person and help in some way.

I would like to tell you about Cheryl.

Cheryl's story is not unique, except to her loving husband and family. However, remaining in contact with her family and friend Vikki by email has provided a record which demonstrates the accuracy by which we can access information about moods and feelings, and treat the energetic changes that reveal themselves to us – regardless of distance.

Please bear in mind that what is told here is a brief glimpse of what took place over an eight month period and is therefore an incomplete version.

I received a phone call from Vikki in Malawi, asking if I could help with the wife of a friend who was going through a particularly bad time with cancer. I was given the name 'Cheryl' and where she was living, which was on a different continent, half way across the world from the UK, several thousand miles away from both Vikki and me.

Vikki and her Reiki group were also identifying Cheryl's energetic 'fingerprint' and treating what they found. A newly arrived photo helped to confirm the 'fingerprint'.

From March 2004 we remained in close contact with both Cheryl and her husband, monitoring and treating on an almost daily basis, sending information to Rolf, Cheryl's husband, at regular intervals and whenever something significant appeared in Cheryl's mood or treatment. Rolf confirmed the accuracy of our findings and that our work was taking noticeable effect, much to the disbelief of both Rolf and the Doctors who had noted an unexpected improvement in Cheryl's condition in both body and mind.

Cheryl's condition stabilised for a short time and then we (Vikki, Stella and I) noticed a change in Cheryl's feelings and moods. It was quite evident to us that the course of her illness fluctuated almost in parallel with her state of mind. Amongst other things, Cheryl had concerns about responsibility and guilt about what she could or couldn't do; her health deteriorated accordingly, and the pain returned.

In mid-October I contacted Vikki as I was concerned that I had suddenly not been able to 'locate' Cheryl; it was as though she had energetically disappeared. Vikki was having the same experience and it looked to us that we were no longer needed; a door had closed, and Cheryl was making decisions with regard to her life – our work was done. Cheryl, it seems had made a decision, and died shortly after.

It may seem to be a massive step to move from being able to treat a client in front of you to a client whom you have never seen and is thousands of miles away, but in essence there is very little difference. The ability to use Receptors and access Emotional Resonance make this step a simple one - distance is not problem, neither is the fact that you have not met the client. You do not need to be a therapist to do this work.

If you have Receptors and can access Emotional Resonances you can access the person involved, recognise what wants to change energetically and make those changes indicated by the body/mind.

Accessing Emotional Resonances provides information that may not be known to family who are perhaps presented with a brave face or behaviour-moods that they don't understand. This can open a dialogue for solution finding. However, care, ethics and responsibility must be observed where you have access to anyone's innermost feelings. You are in the privileged position of an observer with access even to their subconscious mind so must take care not to interpret, label or judge.

The distant client is an active participant in all that is going on, whether they realise it or not. Their conscious and subconscious mind may not necessarily be in agreement. However, the Universe listens to the subconscious mind to which it is deeply connected, and reflects the 'real them'. It is not fooled by logic or debate.

There may be a struggle for supremacy between the two but the subconscious mind will win in the end. When both agree, there is unison of purpose. In a unified choice to leave this mortal plane the individual merges with the universe. The energetic field, by which they can be identified in life, loses its individuality and merges with the Universal Mind.

When the fingerprint you have come to know cannot be found, it is time to step back and accept the message. You have done all you can, you have played your part and your job is done.

The fingerprint is multifaceted and at the heart of these facets is one that does not want to change. This is the 'fundamental'. The fundamental, we discovered some years later, can be located in life and in death. This fundamental is a point of connection with someone who has moved into another dimension.

These connections are available to us, and enable us to have an opportunity to bring closure to events that are long past. Everything we think and feel creates ripples that continue to travel in all directions. In this way, everything comes into contact with a single thought; its imprint is in some way locked in time - everywhere. If we take that theory to its logical conclusion then everything is present, right here. We can access the past and the future right here where we are - via fingerprinting or via Remote Viewing. In order to access everything we only need to be precisely where we are now.

12

THE WIZARD AND ADVANCED FINGERPRINTING

> *Wizardry is about the art of transformation, which can only be carried out if one knows how it works. The wizard works his/her magic with understanding born of deep personal experience and in full responsibility for all actions taken.*

Depending on your point of view, one of the greatest mysteries of life is what happens to the individual, the identifiable 'I', when we are on the point of death.

Over a period of six years, I and my colleagues have had a number of invited, privileged opportunities to experience the changing qualities of the energy field as a person moved through serious illness towards death. Prior to death we all had the same experience with each person to the point that we knew when the person was about to die.

That is, until we met the vanishing wizard.

Like the evidence of a stone dropped in the centre of a still lake, each of us creates energetic ripples that are instantly detectable everywhere. Some of these ripples are as a result of what we think and feel, and others are what we **are**.

Each place or living thing is set of frequencies, rather like a piece of music. Although the music is constantly changing we can identify the composer of this piece of music, which has a unique identity. As will be clear by now, we call this constant unique identity 'The Fingerprint'.

To illustrate this, you may recognise from its style a piece of music to be by Beethoven even though you may not have heard the specific piece before; and so it is with ourselves, and how others can identify us, anywhere, even though we are constantly changing.

In the chapter 'Through the Veil of Death' we tell the story of Cheryl and how the loss of her fingerprint was recognised shortly before her death. Since that time we (the Waveform team) have had many long-distance clients and noted that, when the fingerprint was no longer identifiable, the client had at most only hours to live.

In one case I phoned the lady I was treating as her fingerprint had disappeared, to be informed by her daughter that she was in her last hours and had her family around her bedside. She died within the hour.

I and the team have experienced the same phenomenon many times now. So, what happens to the energetic part of the person that is uniquely 'them'? Does it disappear, change into something that we do not recognise, merge with the Universal Mind?

It seems to us that each person on at least a subconscious level has made a decision to move on, and this decision changes that which we have previously been able to identify. But what form this change takes we had yet to identify.

Enter the Wizard.

We had known about JB since the very start of Waveform in 1996. He was described as a man with amazing energetic powers and abilities. A veritable wizard, if anyone deserved to be called that.

He trained very few students, and he chose only those he considered to be ready and rejected those he considered had more work to do on themselves. Our problem was that JB seemed to have disappeared off the map - no one knew where he was living (that is if he was still alive) or even if he still taught his skills. All attempts to find the Wizard failed, and as the years passed, thoughts of the Wizard, let alone the desire to learn from him, became less and less important.

Six years later, one of the original group of three students of Waveform (who we will call 'E') was treating a Malaysian lady ('K'), who said that her teacher wanted to meet the person who was such a good healer and helping his student. To the astonishment of K, E asked without hesitation, 'Is his name JB?'

The Wizard had been found.

The Wizard was alive and still teaching, and for a time E became his student and remained a lifelong friend.

I had moved on since the early days of Waveform - Waveform had moved on and developed to a degree that could not have been even imagined in 1996. However, I enquired through E if it would be possible to meet the Wizard. The message was passed on, but with no feedback I decided that the meeting wasn't meant to happen.

Years passed.

One evening I received a call from K who asked me why I wanted to meet the Wizard. I replied that I had heard about him many years ago. However, I was just interested in meeting a man I had heard about who was almost a legend. I required nothing from him.

K's next phone call confirmed that the Wizard wanted to meet me and Stella, and a date was arranged for him and K to come to our home.

The Wizard was a tall man, with an easy sense of humour and a ready laugh. His age was hard to tell but he was at least in his 70s. In contrast K was petite, less than 5 ft in height, and she was his senior pupil, his right hand, and had trained with him for a great many years.

What took place during the three and a half hours the Wizard and his apprentice were with us is not the subject of this article. However, what happened after the meeting very much is.

Before the Wizard and K left there was a brief time when he was engaged in conversation with Stella, who had made such a great impression on him. K told me that if there was something I wanted from the Wizard I should ask him. I replied that there wasn't anything that I wanted from him, but that I had enjoyed the meeting very much and hoped that we may all meet again. Perhaps, if there was a reason why we had met it may come out then.

As he was leaving our home, I caught the Wizard as he stumbled down the front steps of the house. Only later was I told that he had been feeling ill that day, he had also felt dizzy and had a fall, but had been determined to come and meet us.

Less than three weeks after our meeting with the Wizard, we heard from K that he was seriously ill in hospital. We heard later that cancer had spread throughout his body and were asked if our team could provide distant healing.

The Wizard's sense of humour

We put out an 'alert' to our team who used me as a 'beacon' to locate the Wizard's fingerprint, and over the weeks that followed we monitored his energetic and emotional state, creating change where it was indicated and advising K of our findings. We were notified by K that the Wizard was aware of us 'visiting' and, whilst he was grateful for our help, he hadn't anticipated the degree of access we had obtained to his energetic field and also his emotions. It appears that he was a bit put out by this, and during one 'visit' by a team member the Wizard apparently said 'Thanks, now clear off!'

This raised a smile, not only from us but also from K when we fed the information back to her. This, we were told, was certainly the Wizard's way of responding. Then what we had been dreading actually happened: I lost the Wizard's fingerprint, and so had two other members of the team. We feared the worst. Joe in Switzerland then reported that he could still locate him, and we homed in on Joe as a beacon and, sure enough, there was the wizard, still alive. This was confirmed by K who laughed when we told her that he had 'led us a merry dance' but we had located him again.

Yes, the Wizard still wanted us to continue to 'visit' and create changes as required, but that did not stop him from giving us the slip twice more. One of us, however, always had a means of recognising where he was and we all zoomed in on the new beacon. Was this a test of some kind?

Six weeks from first being informed that the Wizard was ill, we were told by K that he passed away in the early hours of the morning. His loss to those who loved him and were devoted pupils is difficult to assess but we were aware that K, who was our only link with the wizard, was devastated. The Wizard had told her that his teaching was now in her hands, and she was to get on with it.

Our brief association with the Wizard had been nothing less than a steep learning curve. How had he managed to change his fingerprint so we were, at least temporarily, unable to find him? We were also now going to have to rethink what happens when the fingerprint disappears, as this contradicted our hypothesis that death, or impending death, was inevitably what follows.

The Wizard's lesson

What was fascinating was that, no matter how the wizard changed his unique individual energetic pattern, he could still be found i.e. something of 'him' remained that was not obvious, but certainly identifiable.

If this was the case then it pointed to the possibility that after death the fingerprint may still be there, just not in a form that we can readily recognise. Thanks to the flexibility of the 'search mode' of some members of the team, the wizard was found through something that was still recognizable; for one of us at least his energetic connection was still there. As the initial 'beacon' for our team to home in on, I had retained that connection with the Wizard which Joe could sense, but of which I was totally unaware.

It appears that whilst we all recognised a particular energetic pattern which related to each individual, there were aspects of this that we were particularly drawn to ourselves as individuals.

Three people looking at a picture by the French artist Cezanne all recognise the style of the painting and know it to be Cezanne. As well as the overall style, one person notes in particular the colours the painter uses, another notices the way that the paint is applied, and the last one the way that light is used to create atmosphere. Each aspect is an individual quality of the overall painting, making a unique picture that can only be a Cezanne. It is knowledge of these and other unique qualities of a painter that enables art experts to discover forgeries.

For our team, although all of us had identified the whole (energetic) picture, some members like Joe have also recognised a unique quality that leads us to find the other aspects that have in some way (been) changed.

Our experience until then was that a vanishing fingerprint meant death. But the Wizard had proved that the fingerprint could be made undetectable in life - unless, that is, individual qualities of the fingerprint were known and could be identified. In the process of dying, when all is a state of change, does at least one unique aspect of the fingerprint remain identifiable when the shift takes place between dimensions?

If we find that unique 'ripple' that remains we have found the source of the transmission and have identified the transition to another dimension. At the time of these events we did not know where these lessons would lead us, only that they could take us on a journey beyond the grave.

We have now made that journey.

Beyond the Veil of Death

Our first voyage beyond the veil between life, into another dimension that we call death, was as a result of necessity. A colleague ('T') worked with us, revisiting the past to bring closure on unexplained events that involved his deceased father. He wondered if his father had felt differently about these events with the passing of time and was prepared, with our assistance, to make contact with the unique and unchanging part of the fingerprint that was his father in life. This is what we call the 'Fundamental'.

The fundamental facet was identified and isolated from the remaining, changeable facets that made up his father's fingerprint. We then provided guidance as to how the fundamental could be accessed. The exact details of what transpired, what was seen and felt are not appropriate for this book as our experiences are still very much being evaluated. However, contact was made with what was identified by T as the essence of his father. Communication was mainly by emotions - 'resonances' - but there was a clarity about these transmitted emotions that was almost like the spoken word. Through the use of resonances we were able to access the interactions between T and his father. We were therefore privileged to directly witness the highly emotive events that took place.

Much to T's surprise, his father asked T's forgiveness for the past. T decided that he wished to think about it. Thanks were given for the opportunity for T to make the link with his father and we let go of the connection.*

Subsequent connections using the link of the fundamental facet into the dimension that we know as death have not produced the same visual experience as the first time. Connection was made with the selected person, information exchanged on a meaningful level but it appears that, for those that undertake the journey, whatever else is experienced during this time cannot be predicted.

Our experience seems to suggest that the fundamental facet which allows access to the individual creates a different visual representation of that person. We are not necessarily going to see a face or the features of the person that we knew. Recognition has been confirmed by the voyager by other means than sight.

We have no doubts that our voyage into this dimension has only just started and we have a great deal more to learn about what lies beyond the veil which separates life from death.

*After 24 hours of thought T decided to forgive his father for the past, as was requested of him, and realized that he was free of a burden that he had carried for more than 50 years.

13

THE POWER OF THE WIZARD

The greatest power that a Wizard can demonstrate comes not from the flick of a magic wand; but by gently touching your life they enrich and enhance the quality of your existence.

You now have the power of a Wizard

Your very presence in any dimension creates change of some kind; tread lightly.

What changes as a result of your influence has a ripple effect beyond your initial intention. Consider this carefully.

Your realisation brings with it enormous responsibility. As an energetic individual you can now truly 'fly' as expanded consciousness makes any proposed energetic journey a reality. The realisation and the know-how to create change and to influence others without invitation from the energetic field, or signals received and analysed, is the highest level of responsibility. This is the real meaning of 'power' which, before being applied in any situation, requires serious consideration.

From all action there is a ripple effect that will change the lives of many. We cannot be arrogant or closed-minded enough to believe that, as our intention was (in our opinion) good, all effects within the expanding ripple will be the best for all concerned. I speak from first-hand experience of realising the possible ripple effect of 'energetic' action that I was capable of and which at the time I felt justified in taking.

A single thought or action has multiple and unforeseen consequences

What one realises is that the darkest thoughts that we have about others create changes in their energy field as well as being identically reflected in our own. Once we know how this works we are faced with both the light and the dark sides of ourselves. There is a wholeness in this new perception. Whether we like it or not, we are no longer naïve or blind to the map of the world that we have created for ourselves. Be fully present and approach both sides of yourself non-judgementally and with acceptance. You can now choose how you wish to act in full awareness of your actions, as a single thought or action has multiple and unforeseen consequences for others and for yourself.

As you recognise your abilities, you release them and they are enhanced. 'Knowing' has far more power than 'believing'. You realise that the wizard was always there inside you, buried beneath the layers of 'I', which is shaped by our programming and our individual maps of the world. Letting go of the 'I' is like removing the grime and dirt of the ages from a painting to reveal the colours and lines the artist had intended. Often hidden beneath the layers are subtleties that give more understanding and meaning to the painting, revealing fresh insights - and so it is with ourselves.

Whether we like to admit it or not, we all have within us and have exercised 'Power'. Changing the word 'Power' to something more acceptable will not alter this fact: we have 'Power'.

The wizard is far more aware of his/her power than the average person and this awareness brings his or her power into life and into conscious application. The wizard knows what to do and when to do it. The wizard, unlike the average person, is also very much aware of the repercussions of all thoughts and actions that he or she takes and, like an accomplished and experienced Martial Artist, steps back from action unless it is the only option.

Having seen life as it really is beyond their individual map of the world, being fully present and aware and aligned between head and heart and in full acceptance of the responsibilities that universal insight has given them for all thoughts and actions, wizards know that the best they can be is to be only themselves. The most powerful wizard does not have to 'do' but just 'be'.

Truly aligned wizards are not recognised by badges, uniforms or rhetoric, but by the gentle way they touch, enrich and enhance the quality of life of those they encounter on their path. That is the use of power for the greater good.

Epilogue
Treading the Path of the Masters

'Mankind is your pathway, his foibles, his inadequacies; some of which you can help; some of which you can direct.

Your pathway has a twofold purpose: to tread the way of the physical to bring about the spiritual – that aspect within man, which is so needed in your world. But first uncover it within yourself – know with certainty that it is there; that what you have found is for you, is you, and is of God.

Seek deeply my son, into yourself, find the truth which you know lies there; bring it forward in beauty and simplicity to those you wish to serve.'

How many years ago was it that I received the lesson with those words in it? 33 years perhaps? I received it at a time when I had no idea what was in store for me.

The 'prophecy', however, was right, and the last fifteen years in particular have been a process of continuous and spiritual transformation.

Joy, my Orkney teacher, had said many years ago that the development of Waveform was such that it was now time to emphasise the spiritual aspect of our work. The change took place, however, without any deliberate action on our part; it was effortless, it just happened. The change that occurred was not only with those we worked with; changes happened within ourselves as we made more realisations, and saw more deeply into energy - the substance of life.

'Readiness' is the key to Spiritual Transformation

Very shortly after my life-changing and profound experience in a Rothesay coffee shop, from which Waveform has developed (Appendix - Realisation and Rebirth), I had a dream that I had lifted dusty floorboards in a room to reveal a number of golden chalices with lids securely fastened, except one which had its lid removed. As it was put to me by Joy, Waveform is the beginning of all that is to be revealed and not the end, as the pots with the lids still on indicated. There were many more lids to be lifted from golden pots - this was the start.

As predicted those nineteen years ago, my dream of the golden pots with many lids still to be opened had come true. The lids were and are still being opened, one by one revealing the truth of life, the secrets of energy of the Universe.

It is a beautiful world, and if we take the time to stop moving, thinking, analysing, intellectualising, there is far more to learn and realise by being open and aware. In the end it comes down to us as individuals to make our way through life. Our experiences are our own and cannot be passed on or shared except to a degree.

However, that is not the same as what one personally experiences; it is but a shadow, or at best, reflected light.

What have I learned from this journey of 72 years? What have my insights and realisations clarified for me in terms of life, and the paths we individually tread?

First a realisation that it is not time served, good deeds, meditation or any form of 'doing' which prepares us for profound realisation. It is readiness! This readiness may come in many ways, for example through trauma where the mind is unable to take in and evaluate, and becomes unwittingly a blank screen. At this point in time there is space to notice other things, which have always been there, but were passed by, unnoticed.

My Kensho experience more than half a lifetime before, although incomplete, and my experience at 6 years old gave me insight into how things were. I was lucky to experience these, but lacked the 'readiness' to move forward from there.

I do not know what triggered my life-changing experience in the coffee shop in Rothesay except that perhaps Richard Feynman's book provided a missing piece of the jigsaw at a moment of 'space', and then realisation.

There are different views as to how this profound step may be taken - the long road to perfection through meditation and good works for example, and the instantaneous realisation where the duality of good and bad ceases to exist and one treads the path which is natural, and therefore moral. This is not the same as following a set of rules.

N, one of our graduates whose consciousness was raised, when asked to comment on another student's profound experience, put it like this:

'That degree of heightened awareness comes with greater (more highly evolved) consciousness. Some people gain this through prayer, meditation, yoga and even mind bending drugs. Waveform helps here because it encourages people to listen intently and feel with their hearts.

My sense of time has become more 'real' because it considers only the here and now, not the past or the future: I believe that the past is history – we can't change it, so there is not a lot of point in thinking about it. And the future will be upon us before we can blink, so we might as well call it the present. So, there is only one time – the here and now. I guess that time appears to be slower, because everything just is, and events are not trying to rush off into the future to happen, because they have already arrived.'

The Destination is right HERE

Waveform creates an opening in a world of separateness, and demonstrates that this world is nothing but an illusion. Nothing is separate from anything else; space is just substance that cannot be perceived if we look at things in our usual way.

Each label enforces distinctions between each of us and everything. The key to a new perception is to BE, without separation and distinctions. Once this is realised, your worldview changes, your life changes.

The world becomes smaller as we move between A and B at greater speeds, no longer having time to observe the world we are passing so rapidly. As Tom, in his 90s and an old family friend of Stella's, put it, 'We can now travel to Canada in the time it used to take us to travel from Fort Augustus to Inverness.' Even at the speed of a car we no longer have the time to 'BE', only to focus and 'DO'; life passes by unobserved, unappreciated. When travel was by foot or even by horse there was time to 'be', observe the changes in the seasons, the moods of the weather. But in the fast-moving age of travel from A to B, where the focus is on getting there quicker, no longer is the travelling part of the journey of life. Destination has become the only aim.

The 'Journey' is one of presence, awareness and perception

This attitude is reflected in many of the institutions which are 'spiritual' in their aspirations, but admittedly provide a quick fix for those too 'busy' to travel the journey. There is no substitute for the journey; and no one can travel or walk the path for you. You cannot gain realisation or enlightenment from someone else's experience, nor will what you realise be a result of intellectual activity. Stop looking, stop thinking and be AWARE!

What is it in man that makes him ignore the key to understanding what life is about? The concept of 'doing' to achieve is so deeply engrained in us that taking the time to stop doing and be actively 'aware' may seem like time wasted, laziness even.

One can bathe in the reflected light of others; however, that is all it will be. To gain your own realisation the experience must be wholly yours. Waveform is a door - just that; stepping through to a new reality is your responsibility and only you can take that step - you won't find it through Google or in any piece of literature, only within yourself.

You have a choice - you can get caught up in the world as it whizzes along and watch the world pass in a blur; or you can stay silent and still as if in the eye of a storm where all is calm and serene.

Whilst we may rationalise that the present moment is where we want to be in order to enjoy life, our minds move effortlessly between the past and the future with the present unnoticed and taken for granted - and yet the present is where the 'key to life' is to be found.

The student struggling in his/her mind to understand who is brought into reality, here, now, by the slap of the Zen Master doesn't realise the significance of the slap, and that it has provided a starting point, and an opportunity for realisation at this very moment in time!

Meditation has been traditionally a medium for gaining realisation but, if you are in a state of awareness, anywhere will provide this opportunity - open places, mountains, streams, woods (my favourite), gardens, lakes and parks. The secret of life is there; it is everywhere if you are still and aware.

The change that takes place in your perception of nature is instantaneous. You may have a feeling that you are close to realisation, but that is not the same as realisation, strange as it may sound; you do not take a step of any kind, there is a space in your mind and you are there - the step has been taken.

I remember reading about the North American Indian, Crazy Horse, and that he moved in and out of what he called the 'real' world. To him the world that most people see and live in was not the real world.

My experience is to be able to move between two views of life, a change in perception. Once realised, it only takes a small period of stillness and one is there. In my beloved woods, one minute I am looking, listening and feeling trees blowing in the breeze, and the next minute I am smiling at life dancing and playing. They are still trees, and they welcome me into their company with the flowers and the grass, without judgement.

There is an open acceptance of what I am. I am no longer a human in a wood with grass, trees and waterfalls; I am an instrument amongst others playing in the orchestra of life.

Without personal realisation, the tool of Waveform remains only a tool; step through the door and keep walking. Increase periods of complete awareness and BE in this busy world. You are then not only treading in the path of the Masters, but realising your own mastery in this Universe.

When one touches the fabric of the Universe and realises the unity of heaven and earth, one then perceives the essence of God.

REFERENCES

1) Mastery involves more than just the demonstration of competence in a particular skill. Stuart Hepburn. NLP Master Practitioner, Trainer and Author.
2) This is no magnificent deed, because I do not want followers. Stuart Holroyd - Krishnamurti - The Man the Mystery and the Message
3) If you do a deal with the Universe. Mike Webster. Waveform Energetics
4) The Path to full understanding is revealed. MW. Waveform Energetics
5) Change **is** possible; it is a question of awareness. MW
6) Whether sudden and complete or incremental, the key state is 'Readiness'. MW
7) Ordinary people look to their surroundings. John Blofeld –'The Zen Teaching of Huang Po on the Transmission of Mind'. The Buddhist Society
8) What is life? Attributed to Crowfoot (ca 1830-1890), chief of the Canadian Blackfoot tribe.
9) In the same way that internal change is reflected ... MW
10) Until one is committed, there is hesitancy. Goethe.
11) Bi-location, or sometimes multi-location. Wikipedia.
12) I am the daughter of Earth and Water -The Cloud by Percy Bysshe Shelley.

13) Wizardry is about the art of transformation, MW.
14) The greatest power that a Wizard can demonstrate. MW.
15) Mankind is your Pathway. Red Feather - through the mediumship of Joy Foubister.

Appendix

Realisation and Rebirth

I left the Shamanic training group and also the Orkney Islands a changed person.

My view of the world had been turned upside down; my Buddhist views had been stretched, challenged and made more fluid. Nothing was carved in tablets of stone. I had experienced a great deal. All energy was limitless, infinite, it could be seen, felt and heard - all was one!

I was cast adrift by the group to apply what I had learned, a lonely, soul-searching time. It was a time for consolidation, as the cynic who had experienced so much wanted to know how, and why? And what can you do with it? Being able to see constantly changing colours in the human energy field (the aura) had stimulated the need to understand. What were the scientific principles involved, and what other information would this lead to?

The search continued as the years passed and I embarked upon an area of study which paved the way to a degree in astrophysics. My feeling was that the answer lay somewhere in the field of physics.

One August day in 1996 I decided to visit my Aunt Rita whom I hadn't seen for a while. Rita lived in Rothesay, Isle of Bute which was a pleasant boat trip from Wemyss Bay on the west coast of Ayrshire. There was time to spare in Glasgow, which was always a pleasure as it gave me an excuse to trawl the bookshops for something interesting to read as I waited to catch the train to Wemyss Bay.

I spotted a book by Dr Richard Feynman, the physicist, called 'The strange theory of light and matter'. Not everyone's idea of a good read, but as I was exploring the world of physics, Richard Feynman was a giant in this area of study, and his essays on physics were easy to understand.

The book started easily enough. However, it got more complicated and I found myself drawn to the wonderful scenery of the Kyles of Bute as the ferry glided through the water towards Rothesay.

My Aunt and I spent a pleasant day together, and finally I left her gazing out of the window of her sea-view flat to make my way back to the jetty for the return ferry.

There was time to spare once again and I settled down in a café with a cup of coffee and a bacon roll, and returned to my book. Enjoying my tasty snack, I casually leafed through the pages of the book, trying to absorb the information within them.

Then I stopped, and I stared at the diagram on the open page - and 'the penny dropped'.

I knew why I saw colours; and if I could see them, I could also feel the change in energy - I realised that I **could** feel the change in energy, and I could do this here and now and whenever I wanted to. Within the space of a few seconds a whole new world had opened up and provided me with the answers I had been seeking for more than ten years, if not a lifetime.

I was now realising, and fully experiencing the answers to all my questions.

A whoop of joy rang through the shop, startling shoppers and those who had hoped for a coffee and cake in quiet surroundings.

From here on, progress was rapid.

What I had seen made sense, what I had felt had substance, knowing how and why; I could access them at will. It had only taken a few seconds to move from 'blindness' and ignorance, to 'sight' and understanding.

The return trip to Inverness was a totally different journey to the outgoing trip.

I could **feel** people walking down the isle of the train; I was physically aware of each step they took, and could sense changes in their moods.

The 'empty' space between us was full of life, constantly moving, providing information, each movement of a hand or head could be sensed and identified as this person, or that person. My perception of reality had changed beyond all recognition. I noted at that time my perception of the changing faces of energy.

'Experiencing the movement and interaction of energy is like being engulfed in the moods of the sea. Waves pounding on the shore, gentle ripples, strong currents, periods of stillness in the warmth of the sun, then movement again! Expansion, contraction, interaction, ever changing, demonstrating a generally unseen fundamental expression of life'.

One night shortly after my return from Rothesay, I dreamed of finding under some dusty floorboards a gold chalice. Lifting the lid of this chalice, I noticed that there were many more chalices under the floor with lids that were yet to be lifted. My Orkney Teacher, Joy, pointed out that I had not reached the end of the journey with my discovery but, with Waveform, had started on another journey into understanding and experience; the chalices predicted there was a lot more to discover and learn.

Waveform was another doorway, another starting point.

Glossary

Terminology specific to Waveform

Alert
A request for energetic assistance from an outside source sent to a select team of Waveform Fingerprinters situated across the globe. Team members will energetically access the person who requires assistance and create energetic change as required.

Alignment
Alignment is where there is continuous congruence between the conscious mind and the subconscious mind which is connected to the Universe.

Beacon
Each of us is constantly transmitting energetic and emotional information.
A Beacon is someone who has access to a signal transmitted by an individual and shares this within a specified group such as an Alert team.

Bi-Location
A person or persons who are seen in two or more places at the same time.

Dark Side
Aspects of ourselves, mostly hidden or suppressed, that are unacceptable. Can include hate, revenge or violence through thought, word or deed which can damage others and also ourselves.

Facets
Separate aspects which form the individual fingerprint that are different in quality from each other and are changeable.

Filters
Whilst we are being constantly bombarded with a mass of feelings and information through our senses, our filters, created through our programming and map of the world, only allow us to be aware of information our map considers to be relevant and/or of importance.

Fingerprint
The part of an individual's energetic field that is instantly identifiable as their unique signature. The fingerprint can be recognised and located regardless of distance and the passing of time.

Fingerprinter
An energy specialist (Waveform) who is able to locate and access a specific individual fingerprint, create changes in the individual's energetic field and detect and identify emotions transmitted by the individual whose energy field has been accessed.

Fingerprinting
The process of locating a specific individual fingerprint

Frame of Reference (F.O.R) sometimes called 'Frame Of Awareness'
A specific area from which energetic and emotional information is obtained. This area can be restricted to a single person, a group of people, a room, a building, a street or any area limited only by your mind. The area can be as large or as small as you require.

Fundamental Facet
Within the facets of the fingerprint is this one permanent aspect that does not change over time or with stimulus.

Journey
The individual voyage of consciousness through the energetic field and the Universal Mind.

Kensho
Initial insight or 'awakening' to be followed by further training to deepen insight. Sometimes interchangeable with 'Satori' - comprehension, understanding.

Labels
A limiting name or classification applied to items, people, ideas, actions.

Map of the world
A narrow individual view of the world and how it should function, based on culture, environment, experience and programming.

Mastery
On-going process of self-development.

Preconceptions
How we expect everything to be, based on our map of the world. Also opinions formed in advance of events taking place or facts received.

Programming
A set of instructions, starting at least on the day we are born, on how to live our lives, and how the world functions based on other people's maps of the world.

Receptors
Sensory means of intercepting and locating energetic signals.

Remote Viewing
A trained method of accessing hidden information about an object, person or place which uses something other than the known five senses.

Resonances
Sensory means of detecting emotional transmissions.

Ripple
All actions and thoughts have a ripple effect like the widening circles in water from a stone dropped in a pond.

Wizard
Aligned, aware master of dimension and time, and of transformation both energetic and emotional.

Void
A transitional space in the mind, stripped of everything, even self. A bridge between not knowing and knowing.

Training in Waveform

Waveform is a process that enables the student to learn about the Energetic Matrix through direct experience. Waveform allows students to recognise the natural tools that they already have with which they can access the Matrix. Students are then shown how these skills and their experiences in the Matrix can greatly enhance the quality of their everyday life and work.

Training is in a relaxed atmosphere with humour and a low student to trainer ratio.

Basic Training (Waveform A and B) is in 3 x 2 days modules.

Waveform A. 2 x 2 day modules

Waveform B. 2 day module

Post-Graduate training is provided through 'Pathfinder' workshops which further develop students' energetic skills and take them deeper into the Energetic Matrix.

These are graded according to the depth of content and the level of responsibility required by the student.

For more information please see www.waveformenergetics.com

Contact

For information regarding training in the following countries please contact Mike and Stella Webster - stella@energymasters.co.uk.

Australia, Austria, Canada, France, Germany, New Zealand, Switzerland and United Kingdom.

Author's Biographical details

Mike Webster is the founder of Waveform Energetics, one of the world's most advanced energy awareness, training and research organizations, with graduates and students from all walks of life in 10 different countries. Mike is also a Certificated NLP Master Practitioner and a professional Remote Viewer and Teacher. NLP and some aspects of Remote Viewing are incorporated in Waveform training.

Mike's early life is full of variety. He was a bandsman in the Royal Marines. In 1975 he became the UK's youngest Fencing Master with two pupils winning three gold medals in the 1978 Commonwealth Games. He was the G.B. professional sabre champion in 1974 and 1976 and represented GB in the World Fencing Masters Championships in 1978 in Geneva. Mike was also a 3rd degree black belt in Ju Jitsu, a free fall parachutist and was involved in Complementary Medicine for over 25 years.

Mike's first experience of the Energetic Matrix took place when he was only six years old and, after a spiritual experience at the age of 26, he became interested in Buddhism.

Whilst farming in the Orkneys in the early 1980s, Mike became apprenticed to a unique spiritual training group. The training he received completely changed the course of his life. Nine years after his return to Scotland, Mike had a profound realisation which became known as 'Waveform'.

With this experience came the realisation that the key that opens the door to the secrets of the Universe was 'readiness'. Waveform is a means of developing this 'readiness'.

In recent years Mike has been a columnist for a complementary health magazine and has published articles on Complementary Medicine, health, energy, and the path of spirituality in a number of periodicals. He is also an invited speaker at seminars and conferences on the subject of energy and spirituality and how they can empower each of us in our ordinary lives.

Mike's first book, 'A Simple Guide to Voyaging the Energetic Universe' was published by Lulu in 2014.

Mike and his wife Stella live beside Loch Lomond in Scotland. They provide coaching and consultations for individuals, businesses and teams in growth and development, and offer workshops in the unique process of Waveform across the world.

Printed in Great Britain
by Amazon